Taste Life Twice

Jacqueline Bird has a modern voice with an ageless poetic tongue. Laced in every word she writes is a timeless perspective that reaches back into that silky poetic vault of yesterday, fused with accessible verses that always leave me asking for more.
Chris Purifoy, author of *Vertigo* (@analog.words)

It is a gift to read the words of someone so beautifully and bravely honest. Jacqueline Bird never fails to remind me of what it is to be human.
Chloë Frayne, author of *Into Oblivion* and *Letters, and Why They're All for You* (@chloefrayne)

With intricate wordsmith chemistry, Jacqueline Bird boils down the essence of life into essential words and potent truth. Her work is a gift for those who seek authenticity.
Topher Kearby, author of *Magnificent Mess*, *People You May Know,* and *Watercolour Words* (@topherkearby)

Jacqueline Bird

Taste Life Twice

 **EYEWEAR** PUBLISHING

NEW CANADIAN EDITION 2019

First published in December 2018
Second printing September 2019
by Eyewear Publishing Ltd
Suite 333, 19-21 Crawford Street
Marylebone, London W1H 1PJ
United Kingdom

Cover design and typeset by Edwin Smet
Author photograph by Jacqueline Bird
Printed in England by TJ International Ltd, Padstow, Cornwall

ISBN 978-1-912477-97-5

WWW.EYEWEARPUBLISHING.COM

For my family

Jacqueline Bird
is a poet and writer from Ottawa, Canada.
She has degrees from McGill and Queen's universities,
and a Masters from the University of Ottawa. In March
2018, she presented a TEDx Talk titled: 'Instagram:
From Catharsis To Community' describing her
writing journey. She can be found on
Instagram (@j.birdsmith).

TABLE OF CONTENTS

PART I: *A Lighthouse In My Shadow*

PART II: *The Ache Is A Saddle On My Tongue*

PART III: *The False Start Is A Room Full Of Marbles*

PART IV: *The Distance Is A Pane Of Glass*

PART I

*A Lighthouse
In My Shadow*

Human

You loved me
for all that makes me
                    woman,
when I needed you
to love me
for all that makes me
                    human.

Trees

I am grateful every day
for having grown up with trees
and what's between them
instead of with a myriad of screens
and what's behind them.

For The Record

My kindness is intentional;
it does not make me fragile –
it isn't quixotic or naïve.
It proves that I have known
the traumatic effects of cruelty,
and I've consciously decided
that they end with me.

I am sensitive;
this is not a weakness –
it does not give you license
to take advantage of me.
It shows that I am aware of my needs,
and that I concern myself with yours.

Let Me Tell You About The Beast I Nurtured That I Should Have Let Die Off

I've learned how to hide things.
I've hidden scars (my life's branding)
and family secrets (my life's foundation).
I've hidden protruding bones,
as I have hidden
        a little extra body.
I've hidden my skin
for fear of exposing the wrong idea
and I've revealed skin
when I was convinced
it was the right idea.
I've hidden tears for fear
of giving away too much
and I've hidden smiles for
        the same reason.
I've hidden my voice
so that no one could seize it,
my emotions so that no one
could invalidate them,
my thoughts so that no one
could misinterpret them.

I've learned how to hide things.
I've learned how to be ashamed.

Radiation And Other Poison

When I was a newly
emerged teenager
I had a boyfriend
who used to speak
at lengths with me
over the phone
only if I was on a landline.
He said he didn't want
to partake in the poisoning
of my precious mind
with the radiation that was
coming from my cellphone.

We would tell each other
knockabout stories
and the line was always
as clear as our intentions.
There was a pureness
to our conversations
that I've been trying
to rediscover in other
conversations since.

But I haven't had
a landline in ages,

and I'd be kidding myself
if I believed that
radiation
was the only thing
coming out of my cellphone
that was poisoning me.

A Led Zeppelin Leaving Ceremony

He liked the look of me,
or at the very least
he liked the way I looked
beside him.
He had a book of etiquette
on his nightstand
and I told him I'm not really into
the Emily Post types.
He got close, then,
to kiss my nose
and straighten my blouse.
He told me he'd be good for me.
The lyrics
Tangerine, tangerine,
living reflection of a dream
were stuck in my head,
and I remember feeling
like I was floating,
but not in the way
I had hoped to.
I ran down the stairs
of the three-storey walk-up
and he came after me:
> *You wanted me to chase you,*
> *didn't you?*

I did, we both knew it,
but there was nothing more odious
at that moment
than being predictable
so I kept going.

A Dream That Persists Alongside A Fading Memory

We were vagabonds
that summer –
all pine needle rubs
and perma-dirt.
I pictured us heading east,
weaving through
the Albertan hoodoos
and standing under
The Hopewell Rocks
of New Brunswick.
We blended into the background,
earthen children full of love
and lackadaisical adventure.

We never got too far –
we were brought together
by a Rocky mountain
that lulled us down its back
and fed us into
different rivers.
Our parting was swift and sweet –
we never got too far,
no, we never got too far,
but thoughts of you
travel with me still.

An Atheist's Adieu

You were a walking contradiction,
and I wondered if you knew that
about yourself.
When you met my parents
you described your journey
as an atheist with such alacrity –
did we know there were
millions of you in North America?
My dad told you that was impressive
and that you should build a church.
You didn't pick up on the sarcasm,
and I couldn't tell if I was
disappointed or thankful.

Upon departure,
you bid them *adieu* –
something I'd never heard you
say before.
I wondered if maybe you were
being ironic,
or if you were trying to give
a polished impression.
My mom looked at me sideways,
telepathically asking me
where on earth I had found you.

She has a francophone tongue,
after all,
and *adieu* means *to God*
in French.

Bear Witness To Change

I asked him
how long he'd stay,
and he told me
not to go buying
green bananas.

Don't go picking flowers
he said,
No, no,
they stay alive
about as long as
I usually stay
and no one needs
the extra reminder.
Let them grow
in your little garden
instead of dying in your hands,
or else let them die in your hands
with any thoughts about me.

I told him
I wasn't looking for an answer,
but I like to see things through
from beginning to end.
Things can go bad,

it is so natural, so natural –
I just want to be there
to bear witness to the change.

Colour By Coordinates

We spent those early morning hours
on a stranger's doorstep
in New Orleans,
where we exchanged stories
and laughter,
and a borrowed guitar.
I gave you a worn bracelet
I had kept snug on my wrist
from my travels over oceans.
It read:
La vie est un art.

I wanted you to have it
because you made me believe it,
and I wanted you to keep it
to remind you of how
you had made memories with a girl
who was beginning to remember
everything in black and white,
save you.

The Moon Is Mine, Not Ours

We were more often apart
than anything else
and I remember
you suggesting to me that
we could use the moon
as our messenger.
You urged me to look at it
whenever we spoke
and told me our lines of vision
would tie together.
I climbed onto that bay window ledge
and stared for ages.

I swear I always felt your warmth
until I realised how cold
my arms had become.

Echoing Lullaby

How I loved that
sweet lullaby,
the one
you'd always sing softly
as I drifted off
in your arms.

Only,
its echo keeps me awake.

Full

All I ask is for
a life full of love
and a love full of life.

A Partial Nudist In Newfoundland

We had been on the rock
for less than
a handful of days,
but we did what we could
to know everyone we met.
We held the heart
of the bird lady in Trinity
and cut cod tongues with
the fisherman in New Bonaventure,
before we scuttled back
to the Avalon Peninsula.
We loved the names
of all the towns
and couldn't help but
pull over at the sign for
Spread Eagle.
Our eyes were strained
from the road,
but our hearts were full
of youthfulness
carried on the ocean air.
You had the urge to moon someone
(my, how you were laughing)
and all of a sudden, there you were –
your bottom as naked
as the name suggests.

Friend Or Faux Pas?

We transformed
the floor of your living room
into an intricate nest
of pillows.
We had Miles Davis playing
on loop, and the inflection
of our voices capered
to the dynamics in the music.
I wanted so badly to feel
the pressure of your fingers
in the webbing of mine,
but I never reached for you –
I couldn't read
      your chambered eyes,
your near-monastic modesty.

I hoped it wasn't too noticeable
that I wanted to sit there beside you
for all of my remaining hours.

My Mom

She reared me to be
strong and independent,
but I am so happy alone
that she may think
she went too far.

She encouraged me
to break the mould –
to join everything,
to try everything,
to forgive society its restrictions
by ignoring them.

She introduced me to the world
through its past and its place –
I am only ever picking up speed
and understanding.

She showed me what it means
to be loyal –
that you stand by those few
you've deemed worthy
like a Royal Guard
until you fall down
or it falls apart.

She's the most strikingly
beautiful woman I've ever seen,
but she has taught me to value beauty
that is made, not given.

She taught me to love hard
and that the only way
to do that is to speak up –
a voice isn't just a gift,
it's a key.

The Here And Now

Let me be clear –
I am not intimidated
by the women
who came before me.
They have gone
by their own volition
or at your request.
I do not see them as a threat
to me
or to us.
I do, however, envy them
for knowing you
when I did not,
for loving you
when I could not,
but this fuels me
to love you harder,
longer,
to love you more.

Bird

My surname
comes with flight.
I am a flight risk,
you tell me.
I am flighty,
you insist.

Every time I speak,
you see feathers
falling out of my mouth.

I am circling above you
(look up, look up).

I need air,
I need space,
but, mostly,
I need you.

Closure

I am terrible at closure.
I cannot bear to say goodbye –
the words splay in my throat
pressing hard into its tracheal walls,
battling the gusty breaths
that strive to thrust them
into open air.

I never let go, fully, of anyone;
a remnant always stays.

I collect the ghosts of the living –
I persuade them to haunt me.

PART II

*The Ache Is A Saddle
On My Tongue*

Leaden Days And Pocket Rocks

I was free, once,
as free as a person
can recognise they are.

I would float weightlessly
through my days
without knowing
how heavy they could become.

All of the moments
that build you
are cementing you into place;
all of the moments
that break you
are rocks in your pockets –
either way, you lose
your buoyancy.

I was free, once,
as free as a person
can recognise they are.

It took me by surprise –
that time could be so leaden,
that life could be water rising.

Years

I would cling to the years as though
they were laundry
and I was static,
as though they were the hairs
of a carefully yielded beard
and I was the evening smoke.

Over the years I have struggled,
as you have,
with deadpan eyes and rejecting ears,
with contempt,
with selfishness,
with desperation,
with loneliness,
spoken in abundant bursts or left to fester.

Over the years I have struggled,
as you have,
with the fleshiness of our lips
and the tickle of our fingertips,
with tender whispers and delicate words
that hung like resilient clouds in the air.

Over the years I have struggled,
as you have,

with the urgency and immediacy
of yesterday
and today
and tomorrow,
with the want of something more, and similarly,
with the want of something less.

Oh, the years I've wasted with(out) you.

Storm

The storm,
       it's coming:
the red skies of your face,
      a warning;
the dark, rolling clouds
in your eyes,
      a becoming.

Gone

The man I love is gone.
There is no comfort in a crutch,
no silence in my stillness,
no peace in my patience.
The man I love is gone.

Substance

Mama used to tell me
to be with a man of substance,
but, oh, how she worried
when I found myself
with men who were full of them.

Reduction

Why do you always wear
your hair like that?
(You mean the unruly, wild mane
that mirrors my nature?)

Why do you never wear
any colours?
(You mean you don't see that
I am vibrant?)

Why do you buy so many books?
(You mean you want me to reduce
my input? That would reduce my output.
That would reduce me.)

You didn't understand,
but I did.
That was all you saw of me.

Everything Was Foreign

I didn't know that eyes could glaze over
in two ways at the same time –
not until
we were leaving this foreign country
that had made us foreign to each other.

It was a few hours before our flight
and we had just returned from
a night out of goodbyes.
I soberly sorted through what
I thought we needed
and what we could leave behind.

I didn't know what you'd taken,
but your pupils were the size of fists,
and they were held up.
I kept pulling you off furniture,
you kept slouching into yourself.

I remember yelling
that I wouldn't leave you behind,
and then that I would.
I remember you yelling
as you succumbed to your rage,
but I don't remember what you said.

I remember thinking you had been waiting
for exactly this moment.

You, my beautiful bombshell,
were an explosion gone off,
a shell of the person I once knew.

I remember throwing things,
I remember you throwing things,
I remember leaving the apartment in disarray,
I remember silence and sleeping,
I remember waking up relieved we were on a plane,
I remember my urge to leave wasn't satiated
solely by leaving that place.

Omnipresence

The creaks in the floorboards,
the flickers in the lights,
the cars driving by,
the casual passerby.

I always think it's you, my love,
I always think it's you.

The Fermentation Process

I tried to make love to you
even when your skin smelled sour,
oozing of last night's choices and small deaths.
You were decaying right in front of me,
and I thought maybe I could love you into loving me,
that we could tangle our skin back
to when we had been fresh and alive –
I thought maybe I was resuscitating you,
but you were never even in your body
in these moments of desperation.

Walls

These walls used to throb
from the vibrations of our
cries of hurt,

            of pleasure,

but lately they have been unmoved,

            like us.

Devaluation

I stayed there.
I wanted to convince you
of all that I am.
But as I tried to prove
my worth to you
I came to find that
I was devaluing myself.

Salted Caramel

You told me
to look up at you
with my
caramel eyes
and I wondered if,
when I did,
you would notice
how you've
salted them.

Drowning

Drowning was what we had
in common:
you in powders, in bottles
I would stare down,
but that I wouldn't take away;
me in salt, in streams
that you couldn't bring yourself
to look at,
never mind wipe away.

Full Of It

Our house was
always so full
of people, of things.
I remember sitting
in corners and shadows
and laughter –
not mine.
I remember loud music
and people hiding
in the spare bedroom
and bottle caps and
cigarettes,
and money, money
everywhere.
Our house was always
so full
of something
but it always
felt so empty.

Chasing Spirits

I wore my ugly
Christmas sweater
and admired our first
(and only)
Christmas tree
that was as lit up
as you were.
It was hard to feel
(anything)
festive standing there,
and so I went
to church.
I'm a fatalist, and I know it.
This is the time of year
when I need
to lift my spirits
instead of
pouring out yours.

Probably Never Going To Call Pete

It had been months
since I'd found myself
in public,
having a drink
with some friends;
I felt out of place
and I'm sure I looked it.
A man, we'll call him *Pete,*
did his best
to pull me out of myself –
I was grateful,
but paid him little mind.
I kept thinking about
how easy it was
for you to do this
night after night;
how many women
must have approached you
as I waited at home.
Pete put his name in my phone as
Probably Never Going To Call Pete
which made me laugh
the following morning –
until I realised that
it might not be too long
before *never* would arrive.

The Bullring

You always urged me
to fight for you,
yet you kept one foot
out the door,
showing me you weren't
prepared to do the same.
You made our home
a bullring
where I was the matador
and I was the beast –
I was perpetually
battling myself
for your satisfaction.

Loving you was always
the death of me.

We Were Collapsing

We were talking
and you kept reaching
for your phone –
it kept reverberating
in your pocket.
Every time you responded
your leg started jumping,
your eyes started shifting –
they began rolling
when I tried to pull you back to me.
Your head kept shaking at me,
your phone kept vibrating,
your hands kept trembling,
your leg kept jumping,
your eyes kept rolling,
my lips were quivering,
and the air was filled with
all those shaky sounds.

Lake Ontario, The Place To Go

It is the middle of summer,
and we are wine tasting
in the vineyards that sprawl
around the tremendous Lake Ontario.
We are pretending we know
something – anything –
about the different grapes
we're sampling.
Our glasses swirl and our laughter
unfurls.
There is so much pretending,
               so much pretending.
We can't help but crack up
at the cracks in our acting,
with what we know,
         with who we are,
                with how we are.
The sun is blazing and we are
roasting and toasting
and calling each other
Baby, Honey, Lovey,
as though they mean anything at all.

There are chills in the air
while the humidex reads 40°C.

Our Colours, They Cooled

Pink –
our exposed knuckles
in the cold air when we refused
to pull our hands apart.

Red –
our lashing tongues,
your eyes,
the warning lights of the sunrise.

Green –
my face as she sat
on your lap in front of me;
your face as I fell for
the words of another man.

Blue –
in each other's line of
vision,
frostbitten by promises we broke
or didn't say.

Gold –
when we met, you said
I was a goldmine of information;

I told you that you had a heart of gold.
We brought out so many colours
yet we didn't turn gold –
we just stole it from each other.

The Search Party

I was not there,
could you tell?
I had lost myself
somewhere along the way.
I was tiresome,
I was, oh, so tiresome
begging you to help me
with the search party;
but you wouldn't budge
(you had buried me, hadn't you?)
and I panicked –
I packed all of my things
into six tote bags
and a banjo case,
and I stuffed them into
the trunk of my car
like I was running
from a flood.

I thought I had more things.
I felt like I had invested everything.

It took two hours on
the Trans-Canada Highway
heading east to somewhere

before I felt a sensation in my skin
and I realised that I had just run away
from everything I knew,
but at the very least
I was alive for a day.

Duelling Chairs

We sat on duelling chairs:
chairs that were supposed to help us
talk and stare and care again.

We dug hard for our words
that we'd carried with us all these years,
we picked them out of all of our deepest pockets,
we unwove them from our seams,
we presented them as though
they were old relics that could be ruined
by the oils in our touch.

We looked at the floor, our feet, out the window –
heat crept up through my toes and fingers,
stiffening my limbs,
pricking my tear ducts,
wringing my stomach,
burning my ears.

This

       is

             it.

The words clambered out of our mouths
with gasps,

and then tried to retreat.
It took a moment of marinating
in our disbelief
before we stood to take our leave,
shaking, separate entities
after nearly a decade of believing
we were safe in our togetherness.

After all of that trouble we'd had dividing ourselves,
we walked out side by side.
We did it all together –
we made it and we lived it and we ruined it
and we left it.

Hardwood Seas

It had come to this –
the two of us sitting in an empty room,
backs plastered to walls
opposite each other.
My legs were crossed, as was my tongue.
Your legs reached for me
as your feet fell heavy at your sides.
Our bodies betrayed us
by exhibiting
such obvious defeat.
I was painfully aware that this
was the first quiet we had known
in so long.
You were painfully aware of the boxes
packed and piled in the hallway.

I wrote a note and folded it
several times,
before I slide it across the floorboards
to you.
I have always spoken more clearly
through my hands;
you have always listened more intently
with your eyes.

This was how we would learn to let go,
this was how we would deliver our final goodbyes,
by passing messages meant for bottles
across seas of hardwood.

Learning About Life Through The Musical Musings Of The Fugees

My cousin told me
to remember the bad things.
She said remember the hard times
and the reasons you've gone
and hang on, hang on, hang on,
because they're the first
memories to fade.

I did just that –
I branded the recollections that
still kill me softly
all over me.

Then I see you –
empty eyes and marshmallow lips
and I think that maybe
I still love you.

Your Name

Nothing about you reminded me of him.
Nothing.
But when you told me your name,
my stomach plummeted to the base
of my heels.

It was his name.

I didn't know how to tell you
that I could never wrap my tongue
lovingly around the syllables
you'd been christened with.

I didn't know how to explain to you
how much you deserved someone
who could speak your name
without charring it
with the remnants of an old flame.

It Was All New To Me Until It Wasn't

His voice sounded
unfamiliar to my ears,
until it didn't.
So, I let him call me *Baby*,
and it was strange,
until it wasn't.
His hands didn't feel right
in mine,
until they did.
His arms weren't
as comforting as I needed,
until they were.

And I suppose this is
moving on,
until it isn't.

Loving An Anarchist

You moved like a man
who was unforgiving
and never forgiven.
You had an air of anarchy
about you
and I had a seed
of rebellion growing in me.
We were well-suited,
for a time,
with our mutual taste
for deconstruction.
But
it appeared we were better
at taking things apart
than we were
at building them up,
and soon there was nothing
left to do
nor was there anything of us left.

The Lure Of The Dark

The holidays have pulled me
out of hiding
and I have been regaled
with stories of you.
I had held my breath
like I had held my hope
that you would be curtailing
instead of nose-diving
(I had lost you somewhere
deep in the dark).

The news inevitably unspooled me,
welling heavy tears in my eyes;
I felt relief, I'm ashamed to say,
in equal measure that I felt grief.

My darling,
you never taught me how to save you,
but please don't tell me
that I left you for dead.

The Search

I see you in everyone,
my love.
How is it that
I can never find you?

A Drop

You love me in droughts and floods,
and I am only ever a drop of water.
I only ever disappear.

Lost

There are days
when I know
I've lost you,
but I will look for you,
always
as if I were
a dog at a window,
a coastguard in a storm,
or manning a fire tower.

I will find you again,
as I often do –
all smirks and reassurances.
I won't speak
of how I didn't blink or breathe,
or of how I prayed relentlessly
for your safe return.
I won't utter a word
of regret,
of anger,
no.

My fear mutes all else
(I am afraid I can't keep you).
My languid movements
will disguise my fear.

I will know how to measure time.
I will know how I am losing it.
I will know how long it takes
to lose you.

Prodigal Prospects

All of that coming and going
was enough
to wobble-then-topple
a girl, who otherwise
always landed on her feet.
Did you see the difference
with every return?
I offered less and less of myself
and you kept parting
with fewer and fewer
things to hold on to.
You seemed to come back quicker, each time
with your emptied hands outstretched –
begging to hold
the woman you once knew.

Darling,
I thought you understood,
I'll never be able to be there
for you the way I used to be.

(I think of you, I think of leaving).

The Only Timing We Ever Got Wrong
Was When The Time Was Up

It is so like you
to disappear before
I can recognise
that you were
here at all –

you move too quickly
and I can't keep up.

It takes me too long
to be reassured.
It takes you too little
to be discouraged.

And I am too comfortable
with being left behind.

We Can't Reach

We are getting to
where we are
and I can't seem
to slow it down
or stop it.
I am draped in melancholy
and being pulled
down, down.
You are ripped in anger
and being pulled
out, out.

We are always moving
in different ways,
but it is in these
that we seem to spread
the furthest of distances
apart.

Standing Alone Outside Of A Sequoia Grove

It's just that I'm a fool
on the best of days,
and today just happens
to be one of them.
I believed in someone
other than myself
when I know
that's what gets me
into trouble.

You're the one who
told me about
the sequoia groves –
how their roots
do not mine deep
into this earth,
but instead spread outwards,
intertwining.
Their connectivity
strengthens them
against the wild winds
of this world,
and together
they can withstand

the worst of it.
I want to tell you
that I heard you
when you told me
that your roots were
intricately laced
with those around you,
and while I know
you had hoped your
roots would reach mine,
I did not know
that they wouldn't,
nor that
I was standing alone.

Words Cannot Contain You, And Neither Could I

My spiritual healer,
my soothsayer,
my wise-beyond-your-years man.

My powerful heart,
my mediator,
my compassionate-beyond-capacity man.

My travelling troubadour,
my songbird,
my lover-beyond-love man.

You weren't one to leave a hole,
you were one to unearth a canyon.

Side By Side

We have been undoing
ourselves
from one another
for so long
that when we finally found
ourselves unattached
we stayed near,
our fingers and tongues continuing
to practice knots.
Was it
fear of the unknown,
or the comfort in knowing
you're tied up in someone,
that kept us close
in what should have been
our moments of escape?

Had we forgotten
how arduously we'd worked
to set ourselves free?
Did we forget that
we had taught each other
things we should never
have had to know?

We don't want this.
This isn't what we deserve
and yet
here we are –
untangled and side by side.

Grammar

The past tense
does not make sense
here.

I still write
I am (in love).
You are (in love).
We are (in love).

I cannot write yet.
The past tense
does not make sense
here.

I Will Listen

I want to grab you by the face
with my two cupped hands
and stroke your cheekbones
with my thumbs.
I want to ask you where the ache is
with locked eyes.
I want to tell you that I see you.
I want to tell you that
I have lost my voice
                    so many times
and I know how to hear
even the faintest of whimpers.

I will listen.
I will listen.

PART III

A False Start On
A Path Full Of Marbles

All That I Need To Unlearn

I loved dresses until kindergarten, when a boy I liked lifted up my skirt for the whole class to see. My peers laughed at my embarrassment, my teacher included. I waited seven years before I wore a dress again.

Later, I was unable to get away from the brat pack of girls in elementary school who incessantly taunted the rest of us. I was called derogatory names for being a tomboy. I cried at the school entrance every day, waiting for my mom to pick me up. I remember my parents telling me I could do anything and that I could be anyone. All I knew for sure was that I didn't want to be like my classmates. Anger pebbled in my gut.

By middle school, the gazes of older men made me uncomfortable. The girls bared their teeth. The boys spread their fingers in the hopes to grab more of us. I won awards in athletics, I received the Honour Roll, and yet all that seemed to catch any attention was my physicality. I was taught early that it could betray me, so I learned how to use it.

In high school, being wanted made me feel powerful, until I learned about alienation, of loneliness within love. I learned that boys had sugar on their tongues, and that it could dissolve quickly. I learned too late that I was defending friends who would be the ones to open the floodgates to my personal life. We had become such territorial little creatures, running on a wheel; we would nip at each other's heels if any one of us got ahead. We were called *catty* with a nonchalance as though this were inherent and not learned, as though this were expected behavior instead of generational trauma.

In Montreal on my university campus, I was excited about a course I was taking in Women's Studies, and I remember the words of several of my jeering male friends: *We don't need feminism anymore in this country. We're equal! What, are you going to grow your armpit hair and be surly all the time?*

I remember telling a potential employer that I was a feminist, hoping to highlight that I was strong, competent, and independent. She looked at me saying, *You might want to avoid using that term when you speak to the head honcho. It's a dirty word around here, and he doesn't want to hear it.* I stayed, I got the job, I bit my tongue, and I swallowed my shame.

It comes back to me as in film reels. I remember keeping my distance from some male teachers: one would call me beautiful and rub my shoulders, another would look at me in a way that made me want to shrink. I remember boyfriends telling me it was okay, then pushing. I remember employers telling me to bend over, and other not-so-subtle advances. I covered up. I averted my eyes and avoided corners. I remember cars passing by with men catcalling me if I was alone, but yelling derogatory words at me if I was with another male. I remember hands on me that I never gave permission to.

I never remember flinching. I never remember flinching.

The Tongue Of A Woman

I cannot find my voice –
all I can taste is fear and metal.
I am clenching a cactus in my fist.
I am punching a stucco wall.
I am hanging by my feet for hours.
My head is between the cymbals
of a rhythm-keeping monkey.
I am biting down on the curb
of a sidewalk and I can hear
footsteps approaching.

Every time I taste blood
I am reminded of all
those times when I was
forced to bite my tongue.

Anxiety

The drowning of my chest,
a flood of blood
and
sandbag lungs.

A Home Inside My Head

This morning started
with a shortness of breath –
my lungs
filled with dread
not letting me
gain momentum as I
re-entered the world.

It usually feels that way,
as though
I am always re-entering –
revisiting –
a place that
I am supposed to make
a home in.

I know that
until I find a home
in my head
I will not feel at home
anywhere.

You Know This

You ask me
what is wrong with me.
I want to say
that you are –
you are what is wrong with me,
you are why I cling
to anything that reminds me
of the lifeless.

I want to say
it is easier this way –
I want to say
that you know this.

But I want to say
I take that back,
it was not your fault –
until it was,
and even then
it wasn't entirely.

Ode To A Dirty Old Man

How appropriate,
I think to myself,
that I binge on Bukowski.
I am at first gripped by –
and then drunk on –
his words,
until
I am hungover because of them.
Then, I want only
to unfold all of the dog ears
before I leave that old dog's
collection
strewn on the floor
of some dismal place
I couldn't possibly return to.

No matter how much I resist
by distracting myself
between
other covers,
I am always soberly pulled back
to where I left him,
and I search for him
with as much desperation
as there is shake in my hands.

I Do This To Myself

My mouth froths with questions
that I am too scared to ask;
I know they would attack you
if ever I were to unbar my teeth.
I am waiting for the moment
when your attention wanes
from excited to dutiful,
when the curve of your mouth
starts to slouch,
when the lilt in your voice
levels.

I am waiting, waiting.

I tell myself that I have learned
to recognise the signs quickly.
I panic and pull away faster
than you do, so I can claim
I got to the end before you did,
as though this will somehow
preserve my worth as a partner,
                    as a person.

I find it difficult enough
to determine my own value –
I'd prefer not to confront
what it means
when someone else
can't see it either.

Doubts

Couldn't you see,
my darling,
that when you planted
all those doubts
it was in their nature
to grow?

I Am Deliberate

I am a woman
who is lousy with emotions
and has an ambivalence
towards camouflaging them.

You Are Water

I cannot see the depths of you,
but I can see my reflection in you.
I can quench my thirst by your body,
and I can become waterlogged
by my own greed.

I can drown in your turbulence,
as I can float on the lull of your gentle seas.
I can be sucked into the undertow,
I can be carried to shore like driftwood.

I can only tread in you for so long
before I recognise
I am not able to hold you.
I am only able to be held by you,
when you care to let me in.

You slip through the slender spaces
between my fingers –
I haven't the slightest grip
on you, have I?

Crumbs

I came apart in your hands
and I think parts of me
remain at your feet.

Emergence

The day is but
a few hours old,
but I have woken
to the plural sounds
of loneliness.
After a slew of
miniature deaths
throughout a series
of silent nights,
I emerge, loudly,
to find that you
have stopped looking for me.

Ceiling

Most days,
I don't know if I'm writing
to myself or to you,
but the ceiling is alive today
and it is all the same.

Unbound

This was the sharpest kindness
you'd ever shown me.

I called for you
to come to me.
I waited,
I waited.
I was sitting still,
until you were
a wrinkle in time.

A rush came over me
but I was not
experiencing loss;
I was learning
what it meant to be
unbound
and that they are
not the same thing.

Return Me To Myself

I am not fully aware
of the ways in which
I stand in my own way –
I am stressing, and so
I am obsessing, and so
I am regressing.

Pull
me
up.

          Pull
      me
  back.

Tethered

I cannot let you go –
not when there are still days
when you are all I know,
when only you know me.

Angles And Tangles

These days are so angular
that I cannot
glide through them.
Everything is wrapped up
so heavily in red tape
that my hands have become bound
trying to untangle it.
I have held onto hope so hard
that sometimes I think that
I have asphyxiated it.
I am too frightened
to place my ear to its lips.
I am too agitated
to check for a pulse.
It is all there is left –
alive or lamented –
and I am not prepared
to lay it to rest.

Misnomer

You loved her
and substituted her name
for mine
while we tried to make our way
to one another.
I knew –
sometimes I denied I did,
but I knew,
even when you said it with conviction,
even when you looked me square in the eye.
I always let you say the words
I wanted to own but never could.

You've since opened your arms
to another,
and now I wonder if it's my name
you long to say
instead of hers.

Is that all the love
that was meant for me
or
was I ever really there at all?

It's All Too Long

I couldn't tell you
what day of the week
we are in,
nor could I tell you
what time of day it is.

This is the kind of thing
that really doesn't
matter anymore –
I refuse to measure time.

I do not need to be
reminded
of how long I've spent
without you.

Come Back To Me

I do not know where you went.
I do not know where you came from.
I do not know how to be rid of you
without losing you completely.

Communication

I need you to
talk me down
without
talking down to me.

You Still Hurt Me

The trespasses
were always unfurled
after I consciously
decided to leave
(and everyone believed
me, this time).

Years, years later,
I was told the truth
of what it meant to be
with someone
who didn't really know
how to be with (only) me.

These suspicions
were old aches
that I harboured
in my marrow.

They resurface
with a vengeance
when they are
vindicated.

Period Of Oscillation

I just need to know
if my pendulum heart
is gaining momentum
in its sway for empathy,
or if it is a wrecking ball
razing reality and
making new grounds
for self-pity.

Empathy

I want to understand myself
by knowing that I am
not connected to you
on a cellular level,
but I can experience
what you are feeling
in spite of it.

Human Architecture

Don't pretty up your life for me;
I want to see the ruins of you,
I want to see the overgrowth.
Give me all the things
you could never maintain
and let me covet them
as the treasures they are –
the most resilient, truthful
parts of you.

Tension

The tension
was electrifying –
our bodies sat torpid
as we were engulfed
in a domineering stillness.

Lifting eyes was a labour
where lashing tongues
had been so effortless
only moments before.

The sloth of the clock
(the elongated tick,
the drawn-out tock)
did nothing to soothe
the ache of our new wounds,
though it gradually
dulled the fury behind them.

You were the first to release –
an extension of your arm,
an opening of your palm
and
I reached,
I always reached,

without knowing whether I was
accepting a peace offering
or a surrender.

I Am An Accumulation Of Behaviours I Never Wanted For Myself

I apologise in advance
for acting as I will,
for entertaining trepidations
when you'll expect me
to be surefooted,
for recoiling
when you'll expect me
to express myself to you.

I am an accumulation
of behaviours
I never wanted for myself,
and I've been furtively
following the stems of them
to weed them out.
They were planted (and nurtured)
by means of story,
by means of circumstance,
and they are foreign
to my inner ecosystem.

There were so many years
when my life was inundated by water,
when it was

open to the wild winds;
there was a time when
I let too much in.

I am going to do
what I can to love you
the right way –
gently, gingerly, gigantically –
by unearthing and removing
things that would otherwise
prevent me.

Be patient with me.
I am not fast, I know,
but my pace is quickening.
Be patient, please.

PART IV

The Distance Is A Pane Of Glass

It's A Trap, Or Maybe It Isn't

I would wake up reaching
for the parts that made sense,
as though they were
flying debris in a passing storm
or floating objects in a flooded town.

I found sanity in the warmth
of a freshly filled coffee cup,
in dirt roads that led nowhere
(the longer I travelled them
the longer I remained alone),
the smell of a book
from my collection
(sweet promises of wound balms
and longevity).

I was an escape artist
without a trap door,
a homemaker
trapped in a place
I couldn't make into a home.

I didn't make it out of there
victoriously –
I crumpled into this new life.

It is still an effort
to stand up straight and be steady.
But I am,
and I will.

Things I Know And Have Difficulty Learning

I know that
when I feel stunted
I am looking down –
I do not notice the new heights
I am reaching
in my growth,
but they are there.

When I feel I am without words,
I know I have exhausted them.
When I listen or I read,
I will soon be, once again,
overcome by them.

When I am without inspiration,
I know that I am too far
away from myself
to let anything affect me
(there is always something stirring
in self-discovery).

When I feel unloved,
I know it is because
I have not been accepting of it,
and not because I am without it.

Opening

I learned so young
(I was impressionable then)
that integrity was
a desideratum
when it came to my
personal growth.
It wasn't enough
to stand in it,
I had to surround myself
with those who
navigated by it.

You see,
I move too much of myself
to the rhythm
of too many people,
and when I am swayed
in the wrong direction
things do fall easily from me –
like rotting apples,
they plunk, roll.
I have to wait,
I have to wait
until they grow back,
robustly,
as they will.

(Nurture those traits,
time insists –
no trait is formed
without care.)

There is so much hurt
that hurtles in
with dishonesty –
when it comes
from someone else,
but especially when
it stems from within.

So this is what I know:
healing does not mean
closing a wound.
No, you cannot close to heal.
Healing means expansion,
healing means taking up more space,
healing means opening.

Let Me Love You

One look at you and I know
I want to create a love so strong
that it anchors us in mid-air.

I want to treat you so sweetly
that you believe me when I tell you
you're a honeycomb.

I want to make a shelter out of you,
because you're the safest place
I've ever been.

Your Mouth

Did you know that
you spoke to me
with your brain
pinched between your lips?

Did you know that
you kissed me
with your heart
balancing on your tongue?

Coming Up Empty

You were a feeling
or a dream –
nothing tangible.
I couldn't reach out
and grab you
by the handfuls.
But, oh, how I longed
to know which parts of you
my fingertips would trace first
and where they would linger.

I've never felt anything
so profoundly
as I have felt you,
and yet
I've never felt you
at all.

Lifetime

Maybe we won't make it –
some things pass prematurely.
What I want to say is that
I've become comfortable
in the fetal position,
and I've become used to
washing my dishes in salt water.
I've learned how to heal,
I've lived and died –
I've found myself immortal
within my own life.

What I've been trying
to tell you, my darling,
is that I hope you don't mind
when I look at you like
you're all my lives to come
within my lifetime.

Fight Or Flight

I was the problem:
when it came down to it,
my instincts said
fly, girl!
when you were hoping
with your wringing heart
that they would say
fight, girl!
for whatever we were.

I'll be frank,
but you won't like it.

I understood the part
in their book of letters
where Anaïs outgrew Henry,
or at least
she kept growing
in a different way,
and he couldn't bend
or veer,
or his radius was too big
and he took too long,
and there she went,
away, away,

and I don't know if I wanted
to be like her,
or if I was like her,
but I knew I had to go elsewhere
at the very moment when
you were counting on me
to be someone I wasn't,
or maybe someone I was,
but couldn't be anymore.

Double Entendre

You asked me if you were
hurting me, once,
and though
I shook my head adamantly,
I wasn't disagreeing with you –
I was denying you the question.
You see,
you are a *double entendre*,
ambiguous, twofold.
Of course you were hurting me –
you are the best love
I've ever known.

Dedication's siamese twin is
Devastation, and both of them
command attention.

You are everything I promised
myself I would seek:
you are the weakening of my
hard *No*'s,
you are a sinkhole that
I'll demand to be cemented into,
you are my senses in flames.

Will you believe me when I tell you
that I feel safe here,
on fire?

Spectrum

I know that you can
meet me in my strength,
but can you meet me
in my fragility?

Keeping Close From Afar

There were oceans between
my decisions,
as there would be one
between you and I.
I told you the distance
wouldn't pull us closer,
it was likelier to swallow us whole –
but you looked at me,
laughing:
Oh Honey,
it's just the world.

Darkness Made Tender And Tenderness In The Dark

I fell in love
with the dark, sad one,
because he touched me
with healing hands
that he wished someone
could knead into himself.
He found the places
I didn't know
needed attention
and he kissed them
at their arteries.
I feel such a
low-hanging joy
that many would say
it's a travesty
to allow so little happiness
in my life.
It looks so small,
I tell them,
because it is cellular;
it runs all the way through me
and that is more than
I've ever known.
That explosive, fleeting happiness

of years prior –
what good is it to me?
It seems destructive
now that I know
the slow and constant
nature of nurture.

Appear

There are days
when I wish you would materialize
like a gentle rain
on my bedroom window,
like mist on
the bed of a meadow,
like steam from
the crown of my coffee cup.

Spoonfuls Of Spikes

I fear what's forthcoming but I'm not sure you'd know
        it to see it.
I keep saying that I feel so empty.
I keep being told to be positive, so I smile and bite my tongue.

No one will let me be sad the way you did.
It's just that it drowns you when your hands are tied.
It's just that I never drowned when you helped me navigate
        through it.

They insist that every change is a learning opportunity,
even the bad ones (especially the bad ones).
I've already seen too many and they haven't left me yet.
I am often told of how badly they want to leave,
but they stay.
I am often reminded of how badly I want to stay,
but I leave.

I wish to live in sameness,
to spend my days
smelling honeysuckle and cracked acorns,
dipping my toes at the lakeshore – waves lapping at my ankles,
collecting the shells of freshwater mussels
and reflecting their pearly bellies in the sunlight.

The air is so fresh, it tastes sweet,
the ground is so forgiving, it keeps letting me go.

You are always beside me, here.

I approached the tine of the fork in the road
as though it were the stem of a spoon;
I anticipated the sugary bowl –
I did not expect the spike in the point.

This is what happens, isn't it?
I make the wrong choices.
I lose my way to you.

Freedom Is Sometimes Hard To Grasp
(But It's More Yours Than Anything Else)

I am cradling an ache
between my palms.
It has found its way
out of me,
but I cannot bear
to set it free.
I am battling an instinct
to protect and nurture it
with a wisdom that insists
I rid myself of it.

You see,
I have been gravid –
filled and fraught
with a developing sorrow
I had expected
to keep within me forever.
Instead, I find that I am
intuitively, albeit reluctantly,
uncurling
my clenched fingers.

I am learning how to let go
of what was never mine to hold.

Offering

Every time I do
something for me,
I am giving myself
a peace offering
for all of those times
when I didn't.

The Moment You Realise You've Got A Sweet Tooth For All The Words You Mean To Say

I have watched the meaning
of my words
shift
as though they were sliding
on an abacus –
back and forth,
forth and back.
I could only ever count on them
when I had any sense of
self-worth.

No is the sweetest stance
my mouth has ever tasted,
where it once was something
I didn't believe I had the teeth for.

Yes is the most indulgent
proclamation of liberty
where it was once
such a permissive gesture.

I know it has taken too long to realise
that my voice is for speaking,

but it is finding its place,
it is acquiring the right words.

You're Always On The Horizon

There are so many ways
to move away from you –
I can say this earnestly
because I've tried them:
walking
running
flying
swimming
floating
denying
denying
denying
that the Earth is round
and that no matter
how far I get
I am always
on my way back to you.

River Woman

I am not made of clay,
I will not mould
at your hand.

But I am made of water –
I will change my course
if I need to.

Womanhood Is The Inheritance And Ache Of Everything

Femaleness is a burden
as much as it is a blessing.
We will bleed,
or are bleeding,
or have bled,
for humanity.
Our contributions to the world
are often what keep us
hostage in it.

Something

It still means something:
the endless hunger,
the pitiable expression,
the fear of losing
the person you never had.

It still means
something.

So when you find yourself
deliberating
in the brief and burgeoning
hours of the morning
whether this was love
or something else –
at least you can safely say
it was something,
even if it wasn't meant for you,
even if it wasn't meant for long,
it gave you something
meaningful within,
it was a part of your making.

Reinforcement

I'd told you
I'd seen you
before this,
and I know now
that what I meant to say
was that I saw myself
in you.

You know me,
I know you;
you are me,
I am you.

Us two,
we are full of
fault and folly,
but we are going
to be just fine.

If nothing else,
we will reinforce ourselves,
and find redemption
in each other.

Longing

My
entire
being
is being
weighed down
with love for you.

I'll rise
in every instant
you let me hand it to you.

Movement

I saw you
in strangers' hands –
their shapes
and their gestures.
I saw you
in the faces
of passersby –
their features
and their expressions.

I couldn't resist
asking someone
if they were related
to you, once,
years ago,
in a Russian bar in Budapest.
We had vodka shots
and pickles, and
he laughed at the
silliness of my question.
I curled into
my disappointment.

I tried to move forward,
but I was anchored
to the idea of you.

Some have said
that I stopped at you,
but I tell them
it was you who gave me
the gift of movement.

Suspend

Nestle into
my hammock curves –
this body was
designed
to sway you.

Gentle

Some mornings are so gentle
they wake you
with the heavy breaths
of a loved one curled into you,
they wake you into a weekend
and let you fall back into them,
they wake you with the
scents of maple syrup
and coffee
and the sounds of wind chimes.

There is so much to look forward to,
but it can all wait.

It doesn't matter how stale,
how difficult
the day becomes,
if entered tenderly,
lovingly –
that will keep you upright.

Pulling Threads

I don't know how to write about you,
and still my hands pull me to paper.
Is it the urge to let go
or the desperation to preserve you
that cradles my pen between my fingers
time after time?

These letters, these stories,
they're replete
with love and loss and language
and you thread through them all.

You're the only thing
that ever kept me together.

Love In A Dead Language

I want to love you
in a dead language,
in a way that suggests
that we defy the eras
by never committing to one.
I want to tell you things
that no one else
could understand.
I want to speak to you
in a way that
no one has spoken to you before.

I want to learn you this way,
each word so thoughtful,
each thought so weighted.
I want always, always
to seek the meaning
in the meaningful.

For The Man With Emerald Eyes

I've been asked
so many times
how I knew,
despite all odds,
that my heart was set on you.
I can never respond
adequately –
you weren't a conscious choice,
not really.

You fell into my life
like an anvil,
immovable;
I was metal, heated,
ready to be forged.

You planted yourself
into my mind like a weed –
I see dandelions,
thousands and thousands of them,
waves of yellow
growing more luminous
in their expansion,
in their acquisition of space.

You were a crack of light
in a grim room,
a connection to another world,
a promise of something
better if I could manage
to get to you.

Resonance

Your voice,
so rich and resonant,
such an unbreakable,
unshakeable
thing.

Words march out
of your mouth
like little soldiers
to protect me
more often than
they protect you.

Most of the time,
your periscope eyes
give you away,
but I am still comforted.
You are a man
of your word,
and I am such a lover
of thoughtful ones.

Give Me A Piece Of Peace

I have acquired a set
of survival tactics
that I didn't need
before
and I don't need now,
but I certainly needed
for a while.
My mind did so well
at blocking out
the bad
that I found it hard
to understand
how I felt
so profoundly sad
sometimes.
My memory hasn't improved
all that much,
but I could never
resent it
for remaining in
protection mode.
I just wonder if it will
learn
that all I ask it
to remember,

nowadays,
does not come
swathed in pain.

Mountain

You see me in parts:
you note my eroding slopes
and splintered backbones,
my marble mouth
(too often too cold)
and my whetstone tongue
(even you've been known to
sharpen blades on it);
you see my many-weathered faces
and the trails made by men
before you.

You tell me I am flawed
in my frailty before
you take your leave.
You, on your quest for strength,
will pull distance between us –
then, someday, you will look back
at what you've left behind
and realise
you walked away from a mountain.

Not A Sacrificial Lamb

My tongue is not
for you.
It is not my
sacrificial lamb.
It will lash
and tie
and wag
and hold
and slip
and edge –
but only at
my command,
and never at yours.

I Am My Voice

I am afraid of the patriarchy
you don't recognise.
I fear your subconscious desire
to silence me
when my voice
is all I have.

I am a shrill scream.
I am a gentle whisper.
I am all the honeyed words.
I am singsong, I am modulated,
I am breathy, I am husky.

You hear me,
or you reduce me to nothing.

And I have too much to say –
I will find someone who listens.

Gunpowder On My Tongue, A Match Between My Teeth

Loss tastes like gunpowder,
fear is a spark.

These fettered emotions,
how rarely have they
ventured into my mouth alone.

My cheeks have been
full of explosions.

What chance had my tongue
of expressing itself
while surrounded by
all that destruction?

None, my love,
not a chance, my darling –
all I know is that
it tried.

Stand

(For Alannah)

We all carry hypocrisy
in our bones;
it is just the ratio
of marrow to morality
that varies from
person to person.
I have found that
by trying to paint everything
in black and white
I could never keep
the shades from mixing,
and despite my better efforts
I'd be amidst a scale of grey.
I am learning to love,
to forgive,
to accept between the tones
in ways I never could
when I believed everything
was polarised.
I will not stand with conviction
for much anymore,
but you must know that
I'll always stand for you.

He Is The Bar

(For my father)

My father's version of a lullaby
was plugging in his electric guitar
and playing The Rolling Stones' tune
'Jumpin' Jack Flash'
that he said was mine all mine.
He has never been the kind of man
to do things in expected ways.
I still feel the urge to dance
whenever I hear it played.

He is a collector of stories,
and I have spent all of my years
trailing behind him and pruning
the pieces I'd like to claim
as my own.
The tales are my talismans –
they are reminders of where I come from
and of where I could go.

He is a man of big vision –
a builder of cities and a provider of dreams.
He is a mover and shaker in converse shoes.
He is a family man in a chunky Irish wool sweater.

My father, he is the measure –
not only of the partner I will invite into my life,
but more importantly for who I will become.

Notes

Taste Life Twice
The title was chosen with reference to the well-known quote from Anaïs Nin: 'We write to taste life twice, in the moment and in retrospection.'

'Fight or Flight'
This poem makes reference to the book by Anaïs Nin, *A Literate Passion: Letters of Anaïs Nin & Henry Miller, 1932-1953* (22 April 1989), edited with an Introduction by Gunther Stuhlmann, first edition, Mariner Books.

'I Am Deliberate'
The title refers to a quote from Audre Lorde: 'I am deliberate and afraid of nothing.'

Acknowledgements

To my family, for all of the love and support I've ever needed. Thank you for encouraging me to be all that I am and for keeping me on a path of honesty.

To Kathy, Crystal and Aidan for your enthusiasm and help including, but certainly not limited to, the production of this book.

To my tribe, for showing me what it means to be vulnerable and strong, and that they are often the same thing.

To Cate Myddleton-Evans, my competent and compassionate editor. Thank you for making the editing process such a joy, and for enhancing my book in ways I never deemed possible.

To Dr. Todd Swift and Eyewear Publishing, thank you for finding me and for believing in me. I am so grateful for all of the efforts that have gone into the production of this book – you have made my dreams come true.

To the writing communities I have been privileged to nestle into, thank you for your understanding and guidance.

And to you, the one holding this book in your hands. Thank you for supporting me.